Strategic Communication and Public Diplomacy

Policy Coordinating Committee (PCC)

I0448845

U.S. National Strategy for Public Diplomacy and Strategic Communication

"We will lead the cause of freedom, justice, and hope, because both our values and our interests demand it. We believe in the timeless truth: To whom much is given, much is required. We also know that nations with free, healthy, prosperous people will be sources of stability, not breeding grounds for extremists and hate and terror. By making the world more hopeful, we make the world more peaceful – and by helping others, the American people must understand we help ourselves.

President Bush at the White House Summit on Malaria

December 14, 2006

MISSION AND PRIORITIES

The strength, success and security of the United States of America rest on our commitment to certain fundamental values and principles. These values gave birth to our nation, and govern our actions in the world. We believe all individuals, men and women, are equal and entitled to basic human rights, including freedom of speech, worship and political participation. While the forms of government will vary, we believe all people deserve to live in just societies that protect individual and common rights, fight corruption and are governed by the rule of law. Across the world, America seeks to work with other governments and nations in a spirit of partnership that supports human dignity and fosters peace and progress.

The National Security Strategy of the United States establishes eight national security objectives:

> - To champion human dignity;
> - To strengthen alliances against terrorism;
> - To defuse regional conflicts;
> - To prevent threats from weapons of mass destruction;
> - To encourage global economic growth;
> - To expand the circle of development;
> - To cooperate with other centers of global power; and
> - To transform America's national security institutions to meet the challenges and opportunities of the twenty-first century.

Public diplomacy and strategic communication should always strive to support our nation's fundamental values and national security objectives. All communication and public diplomacy activities should:

> - Underscore our commitment to freedom, human rights and the dignity and equality of every human being;
> - Reach out to those who share our ideals;
> - Support those who struggle for freedom and democracy; and
> - Counter those who espouse ideologies of hate and oppression.

STRATEGIC OBJECTIVES

The United States Government seeks to partner with nations and peoples across the world in ways that result in a better life for all of the world's citizens. As a multicultural nation founded by immigrants, America respects people of different cultures, backgrounds and faiths. We seek to be a partner for progress, prosperity and peace around the world.

We have established three strategic objectives to govern America's public diplomacy and strategic communication with foreign audiences:

I. America must offer a positive vision of hope and opportunity that is rooted in our most basic values.

These values include our deep belief in freedom, and the dignity and equality of every person. We believe all people deserve to live in just societies that are governed by the rule of law and free from corruption or intimidation. We believe people should be able to speak their minds, protest peacefully, worship freely and participate in choosing their government. We want all people, boys and girls, to be educated, because we know education expands opportunity and we believe those who are educated are more likely to be responsible citizens, tolerant and respectful of each other's differences. We want to expand the circle of prosperity so that people throughout the world can earn a living and provide for their families. America has long been a beacon of hope and opportunity for people across the world and we must continue to be that beacon of hope for a better life.

II. With our partners, we seek to isolate and marginalize violent extremists who threaten the freedom and peace sought by civilized people of every nation, culture and faith.

We can achieve this goal by:

- Promoting democratization and good governance as a path to a positive future, in secure and pluralistic societies;
- Actively engaging Muslim communities and amplifying mainstream Muslim voices;
- Isolating and discrediting terrorist leaders, facilitators, and organizations;
- De-legitimizing terror as an acceptable tactic to achieve political ends; and
- Demonstrating that the West is open to all religions and is not in conflict with any faith.

III. America must work to nurture common interests and values between Americans and peoples of different countries, cultures and faiths across the world.

Far more unites us as human beings than divides us. Especially at a time of war and common threats, America must actively nurture common interests and values. We have shared interests in expanding economic opportunity, promoting peaceful resolution of conflicts, enhancing scientific collaboration, fighting diseases that respect no border, and protecting our common environment. A cornerstone of American policy and public diplomacy must be to identify, highlight and nurture common interests and values.

STRATEGIC AUDIENCES

Successful public diplomacy and strategic communication must address both mass audiences and specific target audiences. Certain media such as television, radio and the internet, as well as press and public affairs operations, reach a broad public. But public diplomacy efforts are also directed at narrower, more discrete groups, especially those that because of their expertise, stature, or leadership roles influence the decisions and opinions of others. Opinion leaders in foreign societies can be effective partners in advancing our broader public diplomacy goals. We need to tailor our public diplomacy and communication programs to specific audiences, using the most appropriate and effective media available. Those specific audiences include:

I. Key Influencers

"Key Influencers" are those whose views can have a ripple effect throughout society. They include clerics, educators, journalists, women leaders, business and labor leaders, political leaders, scientists and military personnel. Our public diplomacy programs and efforts should engage these key influencers, and especially encourage and empower them to speak out against the forces of violent extremism and in favor of peaceful resolution of disputes, tolerance and freedom.

II. Vulnerable Populations

Our public diplomacy and strategic communication must take into account demographic characteristics of different societies, and focus especially on those groups most vulnerable to extremist ideology:

Youth – A top public diplomacy priority should be reaching out to young people – the voters, entrepreneurs, and leaders of tomorrow. Many of our traditional public diplomacy programs, however, have not directly reached this demographic group, which makes up more than 50% of populations in the Middle East and elsewhere. We need to employ education and exchange programs as well as Internet and other forms of communication to reach this audience.

Women and Girls – Numerous studies have shown that when women are educated and empowered, they become the most effective agents of social change, progress and prosperity. Improving the educational and economic opportunities of women can have a profound impact on overall social stability, economic development and human rights. Educating women in developing countries helps improve overall family health, reduce illiteracy and stabilize communities. Of the 70 million people who are illiterate in the broader Middle East, more than two-thirds are women. Promoting education for women and girls in these societies is critical to their long-term success and to the advancement of liberty and opportunity.

<u>Minorities</u> – We need to reach out to marginalized groups such as indigenous populations, as well as racial and religious minorities who often do not have equal educational or economic opportunities. America also has great expertise and experience in helping develop opportunities for persons with disabilities; this should be shared more widely with countries across the world.

III. Mass Audiences

With increasing numbers of people across the world getting their news and information primarily from television, America must expand its presence on international broadcasts. USG broadcasting entities of the Broadcasting Board of Governors provide direct channels to mass audiences worldwide through television, radio and VOA's web site. We are rapidly developing improved capabilities to employ the power of Internet and other new technologies. USG officials in Washington and abroad are engaging more actively than ever with foreign media, including television and radio as well as print. Outreach through foreign media should be considered a basic work requirement for USG officials to the greatest extent possible. With mass audiences worldwide now receiving much of their news via television, all USG officials should make appearances on television news and information shows a special priority.

PUBLIC DIPLOMACY PRIORITIES

To achieve our mission, we have established the following priorities for public diplomacy programs and activities:

> **Expand education and exchange programs**

The U.S. government should continue its recent trend of increasing funding for critical exchange programs, perhaps the single most effective public diplomacy tool of the last fifty years. Exchange programs should emphasize students (future leaders of society) and key influencers in society (clerics, women, journalists, business, scientists, government, military and political leaders) whose exchange experience can impact wider segments of society. The impact of exchanges should also be amplified through use of technology and media; both USG and private broadcasting should be invited and encouraged to produce documentaries and news coverage of exchange programs.

English language teaching is a priority program and should be expanded. Learning English provides a skill that helps young people improve their lives and job prospects, and helps counter extremism by opening a window to a wider world of knowledge. English language programs are among the most effective ways to reach young people before they are old enough to participate in exchange programs, and are particularly effective at expanding the horizons of young people from disadvantaged neighborhoods.

Agencies should also actively partner with the private sector to increase exchange and education opportunities through internships, mentoring and education programs in countries where they operate. Finally, agencies and embassies should partner with those who have a mutual interest in encouraging travel to the United States including the higher education community, travel and tourism industry, and business, scientific and technology communities.

> **Modernize communications**

In an era when mass media, especially television, reaches mass audiences in an unprecedented way, United States government officials must significantly expand their presence and appearances on foreign media. United States Ambassadors should be the "voice" of America as well as its official representative and should make regular appearances on major foreign media, explaining U.S. policies, values and views. The new State Department regional "hub" operations, designed to provide language trained spokesmen and more aggressive booking of American officials on regional media, should be continued and expanded beyond current locations in London, Brussels and Dubai. High ranking officials, subject experts and employees with foreign language capabilities should be identified, encouraged and rewarded for making appearances on international media. Interviews and appearances on foreign media should be a priority, not an afterthought, as part of international travel by high ranking government officials. All agencies and embassies must also increase use of new technologies, including creative use of the internet, web chats, blogs and video story-telling opportunities on the Internet to highlight American policies and programs. The United States government should continue to expand the National Security Language Initiative to encourage more young Americans to learn critical foreign languages.

> ## Promote the "diplomacy of deeds"

America's deeds – providing health care, education, economic opportunity, food and shelter, training for political participation, help after disasters – can communicate our values and beliefs far more effectively than all of our words. Yet too few people (including those in our own country) know the tremendous impact Americans are making on lives around the world every day, through government programs, private and charitable programs, and the contributions of individual Americans. These programs should be continued and expanded, especially in the areas people across the world care most about: health, education and economic opportunity. Health and science diplomacy (HIV/AIDs, malaria, avian influenza, military clinics, hospital ships, cancer detection and awareness, natural disaster prevention and scientific discoveries) have particular resonance and should be a priority for all embassies and agencies with health and science programs. All agencies and embassies should make a major commitment to more aggressively tell the story of how these programs are helping people improve their lives and opportunities. Partnerships with the private sector, foundations, and religious and charitable organizations should also be encouraged through events like the White House Summit on Malaria to increase coordination and expand effectiveness and visibility. America should also demonstrate respect for local culture, art and history across the world through expanded arts and cultural partnerships and support for the Ambassador's Fund for Cultural Preservation.

INTERAGENCY COORDINATION

The Policy Coordinating Committee (PCC) on Public Diplomacy and Strategic Communication led by the Under Secretary for Public Diplomacy and Public Affairs is the overall mechanism by which we coordinate our public diplomacy across the interagency community. To help accomplish our mission, the PCC will establish the following structures:

I. **Counterterrorism Communications Center headquartered at the Department of State**, with the core mission of developing messages and strategies to discredit terrorists and their ideology.

II. **Interagency Crisis Communication Team**

The National Security Council will initiate an interagency conference call immediately upon major breaking news that might have an impact on our efforts against violent extremism to coordinate message points. Call participants should include, at a minimum:

> ➤ White House Communications Office
> ➤ NSC Senior Communications Director/Spokesman
> ➤ White House Press Secretary
> ➤ State Department Public Diplomacy and Public Affairs
> ➤ Defense Department Public Affairs

Following the response decision, a conference call will be conducted with public affairs and communication representatives from relevant agencies to refine and coordinate unified messaging. The resulting message from the Counterterrorism Communications Center and appropriate official statements will be relayed to Cabinet secretaries, ambassadors and the military chain of command through the Rapid Response Unit at the State Department.

III. **Regular Monitoring of Implementation**

The Public Diplomacy and Strategic Communication PCC will meet regularly to review progress in implementing this communication strategy.

INITIAL COMMUNICATION ACTIVITIES

All segments of the USG have a role in public diplomacy and global communication. To ensure that we maximize the overall effectiveness of the USG to communicate around the world, each agency and embassy should:

I. Develop an agency-specific plan to implement the public diplomacy/strategic communication objectives in this document.

Agency plans should:

- Identify two or three key programs/policies which the agency will highlight to support the overall public diplomacy/strategic communication goals
- Identify target audiences
- Assign responsibility and outline specific plans for communicating key programs and policies to the target audiences through speeches, foreign travel, media interviews, etc.
- Identify:
    - NGO and private sector partners with whom the agency works
    - Subject matter experts who can explain and advocate U.S. policy
    - Workers who speak foreign languages and could translate/participate in interviews
- Recommend envoys to advance public diplomacy efforts
- Outline current activities and programs that can be linked to support global public diplomacy
- Develop criteria to evaluate effectiveness

II. Basic Information Sharing

The State Department has created a new "Public Diplomacy Briefing Book" that is available via internal internet to update all USG officials on regional and country-specific policies, official statements and key messages. The briefing book should be a part of briefing and preparation for all USG officials prior to foreign travel so our messages are clear and consistent. All agencies should also assist in collecting and transmitting timely material to be featured on appropriate websites:

> - Compelling stories (including pictures and videotape if possible) of how American programs are impacting people's lives. Interviews of those receiving health care, collaborating on scientific research and innovation, or participating in English language and exchange programs should be provided and featured on the State Department's "Partnership for a Better Life" website.
> - A database of digital images and videos should be developed in conjunction with search engine technology.
> - Material should include quotes in print and on video that represent mainstream Muslim views and rejection of terrorists/extremism.
> - Best practices should be identified and shared through agency websites.

Audience Analysis: Understanding foreign public opinion is vital to successful communication. The USG should create a central repository of information and analysis of public opinion in different countries so we can better understand how citizens of other countries view us and what values and interests we have in common. Such information is currently collected by a number of different agencies (BBG, State Department INR, DOD, USAID, some individual embassies) as well as private sector organizations such as Gallup and PEW. Accurate, up-to-date information should be housed in one central location for interagency submissions and access. Information from this central repository should be available to all senior government communicators, and to the new Counterterrorism Communications Center, to help develop and monitor the effectiveness of messages.

III. Proactive Media Booking

The State Department's new regional media hubs in London, Brussels and Dubai are equipped to support messaging and booking of senior USG officials abroad to project American viewpoints.

NEEDED RESOURCES

Funding

The U.S. is engaged in an international struggle of ideas and ideologies, which requires a more extensive, sophisticated use of communications and public diplomacy programs to gain support for U.S. policies abroad. To effectively wage this struggle, public diplomacy must be treated – along with defense, homeland security and intelligence – as a national security priority in terms of resources. We must continue to significantly increase funding for all public diplomacy and strategic communication programs, but, specifically, we need urgent funding for priority programs such as people-to-people exchanges, English language summer and after-school programs for young people in strategic areas, science outreach projects, and new media outreach to keep up with evolving audiences and technology. Increased support for Public Diplomacy programming is vitally important to confront today's global challenges and the threat that terrorism poses to free peoples everywhere.

Congressional approval of FY2007 supplemental funding of $50 million for public diplomacy is an important first step towards providing the resources required for this effort. This supplemental funding will support priority programs in key countries in the effort to counter violent extremism, including a major new summer program offering English language teaching for young people ages 8-14 and increased digital outreach in critical languages.

.

<u>CONCLUSION</u>

Public diplomacy is, at its core, about making America's diplomacy public and communicating America's views, values and policies in effective ways to audiences across the world. Public diplomacy promotes linkages between the American people and the rest of the world by reminding diverse populations of our common interests and values. Some of America's most effective public diplomacy is communicated not through words but through our deeds, as we invest in people through education, health care and the opportunity for greater economic and political participation. Public diplomacy also seeks to isolate and marginalize extremists and their ideology. In all these ways, public diplomacy is "waging peace," working to bring about conditions that lead to a better life for people across the world and make it more difficult for extremism to take root.

ATTACHMENT A

ACTION PLAN FOR STRATEGIC OBJECTIVES

I. REINFORCE A POSITIVE VISION OF HOPE AND OPPORTUNITY

A. Seek opportunities to link programs and policies with America's values.

> **Examples**
> 1. America sponsors scholarships for girls because we believe all children, boys and girls, are equal and equally deserving of the right to an education to improve their prospects in life.
> 2. America sponsors workshops on workers' rights because we believe all human beings are entitled to basic rights and fair treatment by their employers.
> 3. America provides development and disaster assistance to respond to human needs and suffering, regardless of culture, beliefs or nationality.
> 4. America issues reports on human rights, religious freedom and trafficking in persons because we believe all people everywhere should be able to worship as they wish and no person anywhere should be sold into slavery.
> 5. America is advocating greater freedom of expression and political participation in the Middle East because we believe those are the rights of all people, everywhere.
> 6. America is partnering with countries across the world to fight terrorism because it threatens the right of all people everywhere to live in security and peace.
> 7. America collaborates with scientists worldwide because shared knowledge and innovation can benefit all mankind.

B. Emphasize the diplomacy of deeds in all of America's development and disaster assistance.

Across the world, America feeds the poor, educates the illiterate, cares for the sick and responds to disasters. Yet often, the USG engages in so many different development projects that we get minimal recognition for any of them. Public affairs staff should identify the one or two development programs with the most impact and resonance in each specific country and work to drive home the message.

> **Example**
> Eradicating malaria is a top priority in a number of African countries. While we participate in many other programs, we should make sure every high-profile visitor, every ambassadorial event, every communication from American officials in these countries includes an update on our activities to wipe out malaria. New approaches should be developed to highlight progress: a chart at the front door of the embassy or consular office posts the growing number of lives saved; a regular

radio update calls attention to milestones, the ambassador devotes the first paragraph of every speech to a progress report on fighting malaria. The USG needs to communicate in all we say and do that America is committed to partnering with people of each country to wipe out malaria.

1. **Spotlight ways in which American assistance is helping real people achieve better lives; collect and share success stories.**

   Example
   Public affairs staff should videotape compelling stories from participants in USG programs (women in a literacy class who can now help their children with homework, farmers who make more money because of the improved quality of their crops, girls who are attending school for the first time, science students interacting with U.S. scientists to push the envelope of knowledge) and post them to appropriate web sites. A series of vignettes could be collected on CD or shared in a podcast so they can be made available to local teachers, the media, and others.

   Highlight and suggest ways for media to "cover" exchange programs – perhaps by partnering with a local radio or television station who interview participants regularly or produce a documentary or news report. U.S. government broadcasting should likewise be encouraged to cover America's development assistance, education and exchange programs with feature programs and interviews with recipients.

2. **Use Personal Examples in Communication.**

   - Speechwriters should incorporate appropriate personal anecdotes to demonstrate America's core values in remarks given by officials.
   - Encourage journalists to report stories of how United States' programs, education and trade have benefited citizens and their families.

3. **Establish plans for high-profile assistance in cases of major disaster that include strategic communication and public diplomacy.**

   USAID and military response to major disasters should be immediate and highly visible. Special priority should be placed on allowing press from the affected country and international media access to cover that assistance. When events are catastrophic (2005 tsunami, Pakistan earthquake, Lebanon destruction post-Israeli/Hezbollah war), highly visible presidential-level, private-sector teams should be recruited to raise private money and highlight the American's people's generosity and support for those affected.

4. Facilitate contributions (coordinated by USG through state.gov website) from the American people for specific disaster relief opportunities.

C. Broaden the reach of strategic communication by including all USG officials, high-profile Americans, the business sector and the education sector.

1. All senior USG officials should add at least one public diplomacy event in every country they visit when traveling on official USG business.

    All Cabinet Secretaries should also participate in media interviews with foreign media (not merely foreign-based U.S. correspondents, but foreign television, radio and newspapers), and those media interviews should be strategically scheduled at the front end of the travel schedule to have the maximum impact, not as an afterthought.

    Examples
    ➢ Appear on a highly rated television news or interview show
    ➢ Participate in a school program
    ➢ Visit a cultural site with local relevance
    ➢ Visit a health, science or education project the USG is sponsoring and highlight ways it is improving local lives
    ---

2. Designate and commission "Special American Envoys" to help promote American values.

    These high-level representatives would reflect the diversity of America, should represent different fields (sports, health, science, music, acting) and could attract substantial news coverage/interest overseas.

3. Engage more private sector partners.

Agencies and embassies should identify and reach out to institutions, industries, foundations and private sector entities, especially those with a shared interest in attracting people to America and improving America's relations with people in specific countries.

> **Examples**
> - Travel and Tourism Industry
> - Higher Education Community
> - American Business and Labor Communities
> - Provide government funding to develop public-private partnerships to advertise America as a higher education and tourism destination.
> - Build coalitions of private sector disaster response partners similar to those assembled in Lebanon, Guatemala and Pakistan.
> - Embassies should encourage American companies with operations in their countries to provide internships, education programs and exchange opportunities to help develop their work force and introduce more people to America; companies should be encouraged to partner with the embassy in sponsoring cultural and sports programs that foster interaction and respect between cultures.

4. Encourage Americans themselves to be citizen diplomats.

> **Examples**
> - Better links/information should be placed on U.S. Government web sites to help citizens understand cultural differences and show respect for other cultures
> - American youth should be encouraged to learn critical languages
> - Students should be encouraged to study world geography/history/culture
> - Encourage Americans to become host families for exchange students and foreign visitors
> - Encourage Americans to donate to global relief efforts that reinforce U.S. assistance programs.
> - Evaluate and expand Department of Education partnerships in foreign countries.

II. ISOLATE AND UNDERMINE VIOLENT EXTREMISTS

The U.S. government needs to communicate more effectively, clearly and consistently to rebut terrorists' propaganda and undermine extremist ideology. To improve this effort, the State Department is in the process of establishing an interagency "Counterterrorism Communications Center" working with the Department's Rapid Response Unit to develop and deliver a proactive, coordinated USG message. This command center will have as its core function developing messages to undermine and marginalize extremist ideology and propaganda. The Counterterrorism Communications Center will also aggressively rebut and efficiently respond to actions and statements by terrorist groups and leaders across the world. It will actively seek opportunities to respond to breaking news, rebut negative messages and counter erroneous reporting. Appropriate agencies will detail experts to help support the work of the center. The center will be led by a Senior Foreign Service communication professional reporting directly to the Under Secretary for Public Diplomacy and Public Affairs; the deputy director will be a senior military officer from the Department of Defense. Working sub-groups are currently examining different aspects of the ideological struggle, including: terrorists' use of the Internet, television programming, publishing and alternative technologies. These working groups will make ongoing recommendations to the Policy Coordinating Committee for action.

A. Place strategic focus on critical countries in the ideological war against terror.

"Pilot Counties" have been designated to more intensely concentrate our public diplomacy efforts and resources in the ideological war through interagency-coordinated and country-specific plans that take advantage of all elements of national power. Each pilot country has written a plan outlining strategic goals, target audiences, and the programs/means to reach those audiences to undermine support for terrorism. Pilot countries have proposed additional programs and activities that will be implemented as funding becomes available. Pilot country projects are expected to facilitate best practices that can be applied more broadly to public diplomacy in other areas.

B. Identify and engage key influencers whose views have a ripple effect throughout society.

Such influencers include clerics, educators, journalists, physicians, women leaders, business leaders, scientists, and military personnel. Every appropriate diplomatic tool available should be used to nurture engagement, foster common values and interests with these influential individuals and encourage them to speak out against the extremists.

> **Examples**
> ➢ Specialized exchange programs
> ➢ Academic and professional conferences
> ➢ Journalist workshops
> ➢ Embassy cultural events
> ➢ Military-to-military training and exchanges

1. **Religious Leaders** – The unique role of religion in the current war on terror requires that greater efforts be made to engage in dialogue with the leaders of faith-based communities. Moral and religious leaders such as clerics, imams, rabbis, monks and priests can foster tolerance and mutual respect among religions and their followers.

   USG officials should seek opportunities to participate in events that resonate with local populations, including visits to important religious and cultural sites and hosting events such as Iftar dinners to demonstrate respect for different faiths.

   Special efforts should be made by USG officials to highlight mainstream Muslim voices that condemn extremist violence.

> **Examples**
> ➢ Quote mainstream voices in speeches or interviews
> ➢ Suggest individuals who condemn violence for media appearances
> ➢ Feature them in editorials/opinion pieces
> ➢ Feature them on USG broadcasting programs
> ➢ Sponsor interfaith programs and conferences featuring a diversity of mainstream voices.
> ➢ Encourage television programming on "faith matters" featuring guests who offer mainstream views of Islam, Christianity, Judaism and other faiths.
> ➢ Encourage foundations/think tanks/NGOs/universities to include mainstream views on Islam when sponsoring conferences and publishing academic articles.

2. **Youth Audience** – Because they are a sustainable force and will play a role for many years to come, more resources should be devoted to and specific outreach plans developed for specific segments of the youth audience, including early, middle, high school, university and young professionals.

> **Examples**
> ➢ Sports diplomacy
> ➢ After school and summer youth enrichment programs

> Youth ambassador programs
> English language teaching programs
> Pre-college counseling and exam prep
> High school/college exchanges
> Cultural performances and collaboration
> Broadcasts tailored to young people with a mix of music and news
> Greater use of emerging media such as podcasts, webzines, etc.

3. **Women and Girls** – Educating and empowering women and girls should be a priority and programs should be significantly expanded.

Examples
> Establish women's centers that include computer training and democracy education
> Provide micro-finance grants and loans so women can start small in-home businesses
> Offer literacy programs that include information on nutrition and health
> Sponsor business mentoring conferences and exchanges
> Increase efforts against trafficking in persons
> Build networks of women scientists

4. **Minority Groups** – Special outreach should be directed to members of minority groups and indigenous people who often do not have full access to education and capital.

Example
Martin Luther King scholarships are awarded in Colombia to African-Colombian students to promote the pursuit of higher education.

C. **Undermine violent extremism by fostering a climate of openness and respect for religious diversity.**

1. Support Muslim-Americans' efforts to be a "bridge" between American and Muslim communities worldwide.

> **Examples**
> ➤ Send teams of Muslim-Americans to Muslim communities abroad to engage in citizen dialogue.
> ➤ Sponsor "town hall meetings" between Muslim-American communities and Muslim audiences worldwide, suggest regular programs on USG broadcasting.
> ➤ Encourage the development of documentaries, reality shows, soap operas and other television shows that feature American families living in the Middle East and Middle Eastern families living in America.
> ➤ Engage the Muslim-American scientific community

D. Foster grassroots worldwide condemnation against terror; make suicide bombing a matter of shame, not honor.

1. Encourage world leaders, especially leaders of diverse faith communities, to state clearly that no cause, no complaint and no grievance can ever justify the murder of innocents.
2. Cultivate partnerships with allied governments who are proactively engaged in the war on terror. Strengthen efforts, share appropriate information and reinforce themes to cooperatively and comprehensively respond. Host and attend workshops, conferences and events to promote best practices and share ideas.
3. Highlight the human cost of terror. Where culturally appropriate, foster awareness of the victims of terror and highlight the human loss inflicted on the families and communities of victims.

> **Examples**
> ➤ Encourage leaders of all faiths to speak out against suicide bombings; explain it violates the tenets of all faiths, including Christianity, Islam and Judaism.
> ➤ Encourage members of religious congregations to begin grassroots movements against terror.
> ➤ Remind audiences that violent extremism is rejected by the vast majority of Muslims around the world.
> ➤ Remind audiences that the victims of terror are often innocent children and women; they have come from more than 90 nations and many of them are Muslims.

E. Focus on the type of ideology and society the extremists want to impose on others throughout the world, especially Islamic nations.

The extremists have stated on numerous occasions that their goal is to create and impose a unified, dictatorial state on the proud and currently sovereign nations of the diverse Islamic world. The majority of civilized people do not want to live in the type of society the violent extremists seek. The best example is the society that was imposed by the Taliban in Afghanistan. Books were burned, music was banned; cultural icons were destroyed; girls were not allowed to go to school or learn to read; and women were not allowed to work – even if their husbands had been killed and they had no means of support. Freedom of expression and worship were not allowed; in fact, faith practices were so strictly proscribed that men could be punished if their beards were not the exact, appropriate length.

F. Confront Hate Speech.

Aggressively confront speech that encourages hate or incites violence and inflames misunderstandings around the world.

Examples
➤ Encourage tolerance in textbooks.
➤ Work with UNESCO and other international organizations to condemn hate speech and eliminate it from textbooks.

III. NURTURE AND PROJECT COMMON INTERESTS AND VALUES

Americans and people of different countries, cultures and faiths across the world share many common values and interests. America believes in the dignity and value of every human being in the world. We respect the historical and cultural roots of other political and social systems, even as we uphold the inalienable and fundamental human rights of every human being. Emphasizing these common interests and values must be an integral part of all USG communications.

A. Each agency should identify and build on areas in which their expertise/mandate corresponds with a common interest of the world.

> **Example**
> America has a shared interest with the people of the world in protecting and improving our environment/confronting climate change. Through participation in international conferences, interviews, and outreach programs, communicate America's common interest in improving our environment. Make sure all our officials frame their message by stating that we want to partner with other countries in ways that advance our common interest in improving the world's environment.

B. Develop active, agency-specific alumni networks of current and former official guests, speakers, professional exchanges and study programs as resources for outreach.

> **Examples**
> ➢ Cultivate long-term relationships with participants and encourage collaboration on proposed initiatives to strengthen relationships.
> ➢ Encourage professional networking among individuals and share networks with agencies engaged in parallel programs.

C. Greater focus should be placed on three major areas that human beings across the world care most about: health, education and economic opportunity.

1. Health

Further commit America to working in partnership with other nations to eradicate preventable diseases. Convene conferences to focus/track progress and publicize major initiatives and encourage greater collaboration between government agencies (including DOD, HHS, USAID, VA) and foundations, NGOs, health care organizations (doctors/nurses/hospitals/pharmaceuticals) and religious congregations.

American health programs that reinforce this goal include:

- ➤ President's Emergency Plan for AIDS Relief
- ➤ Avian flu response
- ➤ Malaria programs and summit
- ➤ Health diplomacy and training of medical professionals in the Americas
- ➤ Increased emphasis on maternal/infant mortality and immunization programs
- ➤ Efforts to improve water quality and supplies
- ➤ Military hospital ships, which are highly visible and should be deployed strategically to support public diplomacy
- ➤ Middle East breast cancer initiative

Further partnerships should be developed, and medical and science diplomacy envoys recruited to help champion America's commitment to better health for the people of the world.

2. Education

Every effort should be made throughout the USG to expand educational programs across the board, ranging from English teaching, teacher training, student exchanges, medical and science education exchanges, literacy training of all types, establishment of virtual science libraries (e.g. Iraq). Recent efforts such as the creation of major new after-school and summer English language training programs should be significantly expanded.

Example
English language teaching offers youth a job-related skill and improves their economic prospects, while opening a window to our shared values and the wider world of information. By hosting summer and after-school programs, we can reach young people in their own countries, before they are old enough to travel to America on exchange programs.

---

3. Economic Opportunity

America's support for micro-loans, job training, literacy and trade should be highlighted as examples of America's desire to improve prosperity for people across the world.

D. Expand private sector linkages.

Encourage international professional exchanges, ask companies to sponsor internship opportunities and joint professional projects.

E. Sharing the best of American culture mitigates negative images and misunderstanding.

Foster private sector partnerships to significantly expand cultural, sports, musical and artistic and scientific exchanges. Sports activities forge a common bond and teach teamwork, discipline, respect for others and abiding by rules. Art and culture are a shared language that taps into the range of human emotions and reminds us of our common humanity. Shared arts and cultural appreciation can help bridge political and policy differences. U.S. science and technology are widely respected in the Muslim world, and offer a promising entry point for engaging citizens and society.

Examples
➢ Global Cultural Initiative – USG will work with private sector partners to enhance exchanges of art, film, dance and music and share expertise in arts management.
➢ Islamic World Science Partnerships – USG will help build public-private partnerships in science collaboration, focusing on education, youth and women.

ATTACHMENT B

GENERAL COMMUNICATION GUIDELINES

Demonstrate respect. The most comprehensive survey we have conducted shows the number one thing the United States can do to improve public perception of our country is to demonstrate respect for other countries' culture and contributions; this is especially true in many Islamic countries. United States officials can demonstrate respect by: visiting important historic and cultural sites during foreign travel; actively scheduling "listening" events and opportunities to interact with foreign publics and listen to their point of view; planning events that demonstrate respect for different cultural and faith traditions; inviting respected local authors, historians, poets, musicians, etc to appear at USG sponsored events; and attending important cultural and historical events in other countries.

Use humility. The history of our own country is one of constantly striving and many times failing to live up to our own noble values. Our society is not perfect, and we should not be afraid to admit that we face many challenges and struggle to live up to our own ideals.

Use caution when dealing with faith issues in the public square. Government officials should be extremely cautious and if possible, avoid using religious language, because it can mean different things and is easily misconstrued. The extremists are murderers who pervert religion, members of a cult that promotes death and destruction rather than legitimate practitioners of any faith. When it is necessary to make a point that involves Islam, for instance, quote Muslim voices themselves. Also, avoid characterizing people of any faith as "moderate" – this is a political word which, when extended to the world of faith, can imply these individuals are less than devout and faithful. The terms "mainstream" or "majority" are preferable. Finally, avoid phrases such as the "Muslim community" that imply it is monolithic; Muslim communities, like other faith communities, are diverse.

Create platforms where divergent ideas are encouraged and freely and openly debated. Support conferences sponsored by think tanks and foundations and intellectual publications that foster debates. Seek to empower/highlight Muslim voices that speak out against terror and violence, even when they do not agree with every aspect of U.S. foreign policy.

Use good pictures and images.   Well-choreographed pictures and images convey emotion and/or action as well as a convincing story.

Suggestions:

➢ Before any event, think through a desired picture that would best capture and tell the story of the event.

➢ Where should the photo be taken – what is the background? The background should help convey where you are – the country, the city, the building, the environment. Should there be a flag in the background? Is there a banner behind or in front of the podium? Is a recognizable part of the building visible? What part of the building is recognizable? E.g., capture I.M. Pei's Pyramid as your background for an event at the Louvre rather than an unrecognizable column inside.

➢ Who should be in the picture? The principal along with those who are the focus of the event should be in the picture to help convey the story. Musicians? Youth? Government officials? E.g., if the Ambassador and State Minister for Education are speaking at a Fulbright event, make sure to get shots not just of the officials speaking but with Fulbright grantees in the photo.

➢ What is the action or the emotion? Are they dancing? Talking? Listening? Learning? Enthusiastic? Include props if that helps convey the story. E.g., if the Ambassador is meeting with 4th graders to give out books, the photo should include students holding the books, youth reading, pointing to a picture in the book, etc.

➢ The photographer should think through the location for the photo with all of the technical considerations in mind – not shooting into the sun, not in front of reflective glass or a mirror, not in shade or shadows, etc. The key people who need to be included in the shot should be identified.

➢ Look for the action or emotion. For action shots, get a tight shot rather than wide. A tight shot will convey more emotion in addition to the story. E.g., for a U.S. military big band in town with swing dancers, rather than capturing the whole crowd, pick out one couple in full enthusiastic swing dancing in front of a large U.S. flag and banner of the event so the country and occasion are conveyed.

Develop a communication strategy to support public diplomacy events and policy developments. Carefully consider the target audience, desired goals and objectives, and the key messages to effectively reach target audiences, as well as how results will be measured. The "ABCDE" communication process model that follows is an example of a planning tool that can be used to think through the message and the best way to deliver it to a target audience.

ATTACHMENT C

CORE MESSAGES – GENERAL

- As a diverse, multi-cultural nation founded by immigrants, America includes and respects people of different nations, cultures and faiths.

- America seeks to be a partner for progress, prosperity and peace.

- The American government wants to work in partnership with nations and peoples across the world in ways that result in a better life for all the world's citizens.

- Because we believe all people are equal and equally valuable, we believe people everywhere should be free to speak their mind, to participate in their government, to worship as their conscience dictates, to assemble freely and to pursue opportunity, economic, political and creative.

- While we do not expect every country to shape its government like that of the United States, we believe that citizens should be able to participate in choosing their governments and that those governments should be accountable to their citizens. We believe all people want to live in societies that are just, governed by the rule of law, and not corrupt.

- We believe in universal education, with equal opportunity to learn for girls as well as boys.

- We believe in open markets and free trade to foster economic opportunity so all people have the ability to have productive jobs and provide for their families.

- As a nation where people are free to worship as their conscience dictates, we respect all faiths. Many Muslims live, work and worship freely in America and are an important part of American society.

CORE MESSAGES – SPECIFIC TO THE WAR ON TERROR

- All major world faiths, including Islam, Christianity, Judaism, Hinduism and Buddhism, teach that life is precious and that the taking of innocent life is wrong.

- The violent extremists we face in the war against terror do not represent, but instead pervert, Islam by advocating the mass murder of innocents – and most of their victims have been fellow Muslims.

- No grievance and no cause – no matter how legitimate they are – can ever justify acts of terror.

- Violent extremism is rejected by the majority of civilized people of all faiths.

- The majority of people of all faiths do not want to live in the type of society the violent extremists seek.

- The struggle against violent extremism should unite the nations and citizens of the world because terrorism threatens all the communities of the world. Acts of terror have brought tragedy, destruction, death and terrible grief to innocent people from Indonesia to Morocco, Spain to Jordan, England to India and Egypt. The victims of September 11th were citizens of more than 90 different countries and adherents of many faiths, including Christianity, Judaism and Islam.

- Terrorist attacks began long before the U.S. acted to remove the Taliban regime that was harboring al Qaeda in Afghanistan, or to remove Saddam Hussein's brutal regime from power in Iraq. The violent extremists, such as those who were responsible for the mass murder plot targeting airplanes in London in 2006, have long targeted innocent people. Their agenda is to impose a Taliban-like regime on the many proud and sovereign nations of the Islamic world, and they have nothing but intolerance for all those who do not share their extremist beliefs – including fellow Muslims.

- Through their indiscriminate killing of innocent people, the violent extremists have repeatedly shown their contempt for human life, regardless of race, ethnicity or religion.

- We saw the type of society the extremists seek in the Taliban rule of Afghanistan. Books were burned, music was banned, cultural icons were destroyed. Little girls were not allowed to go to school or learn to read, and women were not allowed to work to support themselves even if they were widowed and had no other means of support.

- The difference between democratic values and the type of society that the violent extremists want is stark:

  - Freedom vs. tyranny
  - Tolerance and respect for differences vs. intolerance for any diversity
  - Religious freedom vs. state-imposed requirements of worship
  - Freedom of speech vs. imprisonment for differing views
  - Freedom to associate vs. restrictions on leaving your home
  - Education for all vs. no education for girls, limited education for boys
  - Accountable governments with citizen participation vs. un-elected, self-declared leaders

- The violent extremists have killed thousands of Muslims, as well as innocent women, children and the elderly over the past several decades. The bombings of a wedding celebration in Jordan, bus passengers in London, and day laborers in Baghdad who were trying to earn money to support their families, are examples of cruelly calculated terrorist murders.

- The fight against terrorism is a concerted fight for values and principles that are universal. Much more unites us as citizens of the world than divides us. Across all borders, we share a common humanity. While the color of our skin, the language we speak, or the way we worship may be different, people everywhere aspire to speak their minds, participate in their society, worship freely, live in security, and pursue education, jobs and greater opportunities for their families.

- The ideology of the violent extremists uses a perverted religiosity to attempt to justify murder, terror, and violence. Yet such actions are always abhorrent and always wrong, and the international community, the interfaith community and decent men and women everywhere must speak out against those who advocate hate, violence and terrorism. We call on leaders of all faiths to work for mutual respect and understanding and to send a clear message: that killing oneself and murdering innocent people is always wrong.

- As an international community, we must foster debate, encourage education and provide information, to help people learn and make decisions for themselves, because we believe most people everywhere, of every faith, will choose freedom over tyranny and tolerance over intolerance.

- Despite al Qaeda's repeated attempts to characterize the world as being in the midst of a clash of civilizations, the simple fact is that the international community – east and west, north and south – has come together in unprecedented ways to confront common threats and ease human suffering. America is doing its part, working in partnership with countries throughout the Islamic world to improve the lives of Muslims. America is the largest bilateral donor of food and health aid to the Palestinian people. Americans were the largest providers of help to Muslims affected by the tsunami in Indonesia and the earthquake in Pakistan. We provide funds for Muslim girls and boys to go to school, for Muslim women to learn English, and for Muslim young people to get training for jobs.

And in Afghanistan and Iraq, we are working in partnership with democratically elected Muslim leaders to provide freedom and security for Muslim populations that were brutally repressed under the Taliban and Saddam Hussein.

- As we look forward, we seek to work in a spirit of partnership with people and nations across the world to confront this ideology of hate and foster a climate of hope and opportunity. The U.S. is far from perfect, yet we believe the noble ideals of freedom and justice that guide us are right and true for human beings everywhere. We want to work in partnership with nations throughout the world in ways that will result in a more peaceful and prosperous world, and a better life for all people.

ATTACHMENT D

ADDITIONAL COMMUNICATION VEHICLES

USG Broadcasting

Consistent with the BBG's statutory mandate to operate in accordance with the highest standards of professional journalism and to safeguard the editorial integrity and independence of its broadcast organizations, as well as the BBG Strategic Plan for 2008-2013, the Broadcasting Board of Governors shall:

- Review existing strategies and resources in order to focus BBG efforts on the critical priority countries for U.S. foreign policy. Means of signal delivery (television, FM radio, internet, etc.) should vary according to audience demographics, media habits, trends, etc. Decisions should be made on the basis of thorough audience research and U.S. national priorities.
- Build upon BBG's reach and impact within the Islamic World, including augmentation of news gathering, reporting and programming for Alhurra TV and Radio Sawa, Radio Farda, etc.
- BBG's various programs should broaden and deepen overall coverage of Islam and foster interfaith dialogue, including discussion of Islam and modernity and Islam and democracy, ensuring the participation of mainstream Muslim voices.
- Help audiences in authoritarian countries understand the principles and practices of democratic, free and just societies.
- Engage the world in a conversation about America, including the presentation of accurate and comprehensive information to counter misinformation and disinformation about the United States, its policies, and culture, as well as the use of interactive dialogues with key audiences, such as youth.
- Broaden cooperation with U.S. public diplomacy, including playing an active role in the interagency strategic planning; facilitating the exchange of relevant data, including survey results and polling data, with other government agencies; and developing partnerships with like-minded institutes and foundations outside the government. BBG should consider covering newsworthy events sponsored by government agencies, such as exchange programs, health care, scientific collaboration, and education initiatives.

Non-BBG Activities:

Narrowcasting: In response to changing user habits and the dramatically different media landscape, new web-based approaches must be developed and expanded by all agencies. The interagency community should collaborate with technology professionals to identify recommendations on current trends and the most effective ways of reaching youth audiences.

Examples
- **Internet Outreach:** Pod casts, web chats, SMS text messaging, blogs, and other web-based programs are being developed and expanded to share U.S. foreign policy messages with audiences around the world. Additional capacity has been added to broadcast live events, such as the President's State of the Union address, in more languages worldwide.
- **Digital Outreach Team:** A new unit at the State Department engages on blogs and web chats in Arabic to correct misrepresentations of U.S. policy.
- **Democracy Dialogues:** A new interactive, web-based discussion of the principles of democracy has been launched. Every two months, a different theme is featured.
- **"Partnership for a Better Life:"** A website to provide a visual gateway to stories of individuals and institutions benefiting from U.S. foreign aid has been established, building on President Bush's State of the Union message that: "For people everywhere, America is a partner for a better life." Our ambassadors are strongly encouraged to highlight ways the American government and people are improving the lives of people in their host countries.

ATTACHMENT E

EVALUATION AND ACCOUNTABILITY

As Edward R. Murrow once observed, no cash register ever rings when a mind is changed. The impact of information and education programs that touch the emotions, beliefs, intellects and allegiances of diverse audiences around the world is often difficult to gauge, especially when many public diplomacy activities may only produce long-term, rather than immediate, impact.

Nevertheless, all United States government agencies must build evaluation and measurement into strategic communication and public diplomacy program design. They must examine the effectiveness and impact of their efforts. While we cannot prove that additional USG appearances on television will change minds, we can track the growing number of interviews, the time allotted to representing America's point of view, and whether our key messages were in fact conveyed. Participants in our exchange and education programs can and should be interviewed to find out what aspects were most effective; speakers should be evaluated for quality and effectiveness in presenting American values and beliefs.

Evaluation should measure progress toward the achievement of goals, allowing managers to adjust methods and means, and make informed decisions about resources. Performance measurement and evaluation ensure accountability and transparency so that stakeholders, including the American public, can justify program expenditures as a prudent use of taxpayer funds.

The Policy Coordinating Committee should implement its evaluation and measurement strategy as follows:

- **Establish a culture of measurement:** The PCC will communicate to all departments and agencies the importance and value of evaluations and performance measurement using common standards and comparable data that support the three strategic imperatives. Increased commitment to data collection and reporting will help improve communication and public diplomacy programming and more effectively demonstrate the impact of our collective efforts.

- **Establish common core performance indicators:** The PCC will analyze the performance indicators submitted by departments and agencies with a view to approve a uniform set of relevant core indicators for use in all agencies. Individual agencies will then create sub-indictors to comprehensively evaluate supporting internal efforts. This will provide greater focus and coherence across agencies and bureaus, standardize and streamline processes for the field, and ensure data collection supports both processes.

- **Establish mechanisms for data collection:** Each individual agency and department shall allocate resources, establish indicators, and deploy mechanisms to gather relevant data. This evaluation process will be used to establish baselines and track the impact of public diplomacy programs and activities.

- **The PCC will conduct periodic agency-specific reviews** of public diplomacy and strategic communication efforts to validate successful programs, recommend the continuation of activities, and direct resources.